INNER THOUGHTS

Maxime Appoléon

TO « N »

« Have faith in your journey

Everything had to happen exactly as it did to get you were you are next

You'll breathe

You'll think of solutions

You'll not let your worries controls you

You'll simply breathe and it will be alright because you don't and never quit

Because you are a strong person »

JOURNEY

When you take me to the sky
You're pulling me in a world
Where I am flying high

With you I am always willing to share
The secret passion bursting in the air

When I keep you in my arms
Your fragrance is filling like a drug
To touch you I can't get enough
Ecstacy is screaming in my head

I hope you'll keep me in your heart
For you couldn't return this love
In your heart, try not to forget me much
For, in mine you'll never be gone.

FEELINGS

Tell me about the extent of what you are hiding
from me

What worries you

From inside to outside

From hidden to revealed

From your being to my being

Hearing the sound of your voice

Contemplating your face and your smile
transported me to a sphere

Where time was eternal and

Where eloquent silence reigned outside

I've never seen you so brave, being so intimate

You agreed to tell me what you had experienced in
your life

You made me understand it with strong enough
words, fiery gestures and glances

At that precise moment, I was only feeling
empathy and love for you

The idea of hugging you, comforting you, to let our
beating hearts is be heard invaded my head

REGRETS

I wish I could tell you more that I was sorry

I broke your heart and mine at the same time

I would have liked to hug you one last time,

Love you a little more, before saying goodbye

I would have preferred to admit that I couldn't
move forward without you, rather than let the
words die in me

I would have liked to shout at you not to leave,

Tell you to wait for me because I still need you

I wish I had told you a little earlier that I still loved
you

And I had never stop doing it despite all the harm I have done to you

I would have liked to drown our past in an even more joyful

And unsinkable present

TEACH ME LOVE

I am a loner

Always have been one

Now that I am older

There is nothing that can be done

But then our path crossed

And away all my faith you tossed

Show me what is to love

So I can feel it too

Give me a way to improve

And in time I'll share it with you

Sometimes, I'll mess up

Sometimes, I'll give up

But never it will be enough

So I'll always keep on trying

I feel pressure

In every place I've been gone

As a lover

I oath to be alone

But then you came over and whirled my entire world

Tell me what is that you feel

Tell me how do you keep it real

What is making you stand

How does you heart pound

Show me what is to love

So I can feel it too

Give me a way to improve

And in time I'll share it with you

DISTORTED

I made it distorted

This love I distorted

When I slip deep in the dark

I always hope you'll be my light

From daylight to moonlight

You make me see stars

When I am lost

It's you I find

From the very start

You were always in my mind

Even if in your eyes I am unmaterial

In your hands I come alive

But that's when it gets complicated

When Love is only in one way

When you gaze at me

Your eyes may be empty

But mine you see

Are full of envy

It may be true you hold no love for me

I'll hold on because in reality

Before you there were empty years

After you eternity would be hard to bear

BLACK HOLE

I see through your face

An unknown kind of distress

From your eyes, like a black hole

Not even the light can come out of it

Hanging from the tip of your lips

Some kind of tears

You may remain mysterious

But the twitch of your muscle

Gives you away

You may seem calm and serene

But in the depth of your black stare

I see the fire in there

A glittering shrill in the silence

A dangerous mix of fragrance

You buried to much

You little body, a dwarf

From excuses, you sulked

From hated, you morphed

WITHOUT PAUSE

Why are you not sleeping ?

You seem restless

I know that time is running out

And Life is limited

But if you don't slow down

You'll never have you rest

You know what is your quest

You want to live a life

Without pause

Why can't you keep still ?

You seem in a frenzy

Like in your mind

There was an earthquake

I know that time is running out

And Life is limited

Even in relapse

You want to live a life

Without pause

You despair to see, know and save

Things come unquantified

But in the blink of an eye

You're already in the past

APOLOGIES

I misconducted myself
And for this I give you
All my apologize

Let's start all over again
I beg you
Cause now I know
Where I want to go with you

You used to complain
I was never here for you
Hard to live with someone
Who lives like he's all alone

For you, It was critical
For me, It was not simple

I misconducted myself

And for this I give you

All my apologize

Let's start all over again

I beg you

Cause now I know

Where I want to go with you

When I act cold

You kept me warm

Nonetheless it didn't stop me

From feeling alone

In between our problems

Things were less the same

I misconducted myself

And for this I give you

All my apologize

Let's start all over again

I beg you

Cause now I know

Where I want to go with you

Acting cold and distant

Was the only way I knew

When loving and communicate

Was the only thing I had to do

It is hard to communicate

Harder to confess

Ones love

It's difficult to have
A relationship in silence
Now I know that

I realized all my past mistakes
And this old version of me
No longer exists

I misconducted myself
And for this I give you
All my apologize

Let's start all over again
I beg you
Cause now I know
Where I want to go with you

TASTE OF PEACE

Don't be afraid

To close your eyes

There is only truth

In the silence

Relax yourself

Don't be so tense

For all your fears

Darkness will overcome

You'll find that there

You can be who you are

When looking in the mirror

The bites don't sting anymore

So you can open eyes

You'll see past the mystery

In a way, a paradise

You'll find it sweet

LEAVE YOU

I'd leave your good

If I could

But I have no common sense

I'd leave you out of sight

And I should

But I'm not blind

If you weren't so demanding

So controlling, I would leave by my side

But you're naturally incurable

So I must leave right on time

I have to leave you

But what can I do

I have to see you

You know I would

Still it breaks me

I'd switch meds

Had I know

But I'm still clueless

I'd skip the gates

If I wasn't that drawn

But I'm that deranged

If you weren't so irresistible

So selfishly endearing, I would not be this mad

But you're naturally unsuitable

So I must leave before trouble gets bad

BICKERING

Why are we fighting again ?
We really should stop the bickering
End the talking, gimme your hands instead
We will compromise, we have to

As we said it before
There's no way we could make it work
But here we are again
Knocking at each other's door

Gimme the lead just you wait
Sometimes you're right then you make mistakes
I am not insulting still you make amends
We often find ourselves on a thin line

I don't know what it means for us

I am just saying it how I see it

As we said it before

There's no way we could make it work

But here we are again

Knocking at each other's door

Leave or Love,

Love or Live,

Live to Love,

Love don't leave,

We said it before

No matter what we believe

For us

It's hard to break the knot

ABANDON

I abandon

That's what I do

Before it even start

Why I even try,

It's a wonder

Because I loose

Everytime I loose

I am weak you know

I don't deserve love

Because I hate myself

I can't find my worth

I am young but I am lifeless

I have nothing for myself

But the dreams I hold to fulfill

The emotions I long to feel

I try to find them in any fairy tales

The climax, the after waves

Everything but the shame

I feel every time I peer at my reflect

Now I confess to you

I abandon

That's what I do

Before it even start

Why I even try,

It's a wonder

Because I loose

Everytime I loose

If only I could fade

I would be a good riddance

I'm dying inside bad

I am smoking my last resistance

But i'm holding on
So I'll keep breathing air
Until my lungs can't tune a song

Now I regret telling you

I abandon
That's what I do

BETTER TIMES

Saw nothing clear
I once had to turn away
A reflect little too deep
Maybe it wasn't my destiny

I am still looking at my portrait
It is always a difficult task to achieve
I had to have it the hard way

I was so excited, so excited
To start somewhere, new,
All rewinded, all rewinded
I though I'd have better times

But right before my eyes
I let my whole world crumbling

And I came to realize
The deep trouble of my mind

I don't know what I'm made of
I still hope to have it all on track
But I feel so low and black
And to the roots I always come back

Because I don't understand
The things so,
I am stuck right at the start of a familiar wall
I am lost beyond comprehension
I dread that now it's getting critical

So I am lost
Amongst the others around me
Patience is hard to satisfy
Since I am lost truly
I am afraid of what it'll costs me

I just want to find my way

On the unattainable road of boundings

Sharing, touching and loving , to express

Had always been hard and intense

But that's something I crave to experience

Once in my life

So that,

Tomorrow, I'd happy to die

I LOVE YOU

I Love you

You have seen me at my worst

Yet Still Love me

You know how to cheer me up

I can trust you with anything

You are always be there for me

I love because you are my person

I love you because you're my everything

And did I tell you

I love you because I love you

INNER THOUGHTS

(Second Part)

How long did I spend waiting for someone who was better to return without me ?

How many times haven't I wanted to get up

Because I didn't want to move on in a life

Where you weren't ?

How many tears have I wiped from the remorse that gnaws at me ?

How many times have I wanted to scream your name ?

ANOTHER BLUES

I took a step back again
And I fell down,
The world collapsed beneath my feet
I couldn't hear a sound

But the song near and nearer
The waves coursing through me
The rhythm became clear and clearer
And I knew a blues that will be

Here again I listen to drama
That I knew by heart
I need to step out of the canvas
To unravel the pearl

Cause the song near and nearer

The waves coursing through me

The rhythm became clear and clearer

And I knew a blues that will be

Stronger,

It got passed the time

Longer,

It went through rewind

ONE AMONGST OTHERS

Where the top of pretense is

The ring of the circus is crowded

Where a fascinating show begins

Is there someone who doesn't applause it ?

On the left

A performing animal tamed

Everyone claps their hands

On the right,

A tamer delighted

Everyone shake their heads

If you choose to be one amongst others

Follow social code's orders

But won't you have regrets

By denying yourself

If you think through others lives

Won't you see that
Somehow you've been blind

You, in the middle performng
A clown for a fun fair
A happy man withtout character
Everyone is clapping

On the left
A performing animal tamed
Everyone claps their hands
On the right,

A tamer delighted
So much bodies shake their heads

Left amongst the others

CHOKING ON MY SELF HATRED

It hurts to be me,

In reality,

To feel miserable

To come to loath

My only shell

Is my secret hell

I hate myself

So much I refuse

To look at my reflection

Maybe my own imperfections

It is an abuse

A punishment to see

All this ugliness
An abonimation to me
I confess achingly

Beauty Ogress
Is the thing
Fat and obsolete
Farts and unpleasantness

Getting no interests
Nonsoever, being hopeless

As in forever
So much that
The only option left
Is to die now or never

Because everyday

It seems like I am dying

More than ever

And for once I want

To get rid of this weight

On my shoulders

All my hopes

I'd let them burn

On their own

They're too heavy

To tug them along

In this chest

They're already gone

Because they leave me empty

When they turn to aches

As I thought I had them

In the tinniest of my palms

Disillusion on the crest

And each time

I'm choking on my own weakness

Each lame rime

I'm choking on my self hatred

So to hope

I bid my farewell

KILL ME

Kill me in the kitchen
Kill me whenever you love it
Kill me in a vast plain
Kill me wherever you want it

You don't have to worry much
It won't cost your life, but your love
This is a claim for your surrender
So please end the wait and sorrow

When you keep me in your arms
Your scent is filling like a drug
To touch you I can't get enough
Ecstasy's screaming in my head

So kill me now before I bleed

When you take me to the sky

You're pulling me in a world
Where I am flying high

With you I am always willing to share
The secret passion bursting in the air

I hope you'll keep me in your heart
For you couldn't return this love
In your heart, try not to forget me much
For, mine you'll never be gone

When you take me to the sky
You're pulling me in a world
Where I am flying high
With you I am always willing to share
The secret passion bursting in the air

I'll shot myself If I have to
This is how much I love you
So kill me now
Because I'll die for you

LITTLE SOLDIER

A new day is rising
The sun's rays are flooding the streets
From their gentle heat

Giving some conforts in the little heart
Of the little child soldier
Who's only just got up

Lighting up his cold-chilled soul
Hardened by the battles
More and more bloody
Destroying all of his childhood dreams

Go little soldier
Don't hold back
Cause you're holding hope
In your tiny hands

Cry for your brothers
Cry for your lost land
Cry for all the things you hand to suffer
But couldn't stand

Cut all your ropes
And free your mind
You know, sacrifice
Is a useless fate

His sweet smiling brother left him days ago
Him who has just only turned eight
Died in a pool of blood
His body hammered
His eyes torn into pieces

Screams and gun's shots all around him
He went away, nevertheless
His life was just beginning

Standing up in front of the lush brush
His smooth hands are shaking
His sore eyes are shining
With apprehension

His frail heart is beating
Noisily as a drum
The twelve strokes of midnight
The end, he knew, would be today

POISON

Degeneracy illness

Come out of your closet

Come here and confess

Unkempt little boxes

With dark contents

Your safety coaxed

Out of balance

You're everything and nothing

You're not me, and I am not you

Still you linger, you're spreading

Swallowing, you know you're winning

Poisonous illness

Going with the flow

Coming like blows

Dangerously depressed

You don't threat

Slowing me back

You sate your pace

You're everything and nothing

You're not me, and I am not you

Still you linger, you're spreading

Swallowing, you know you're winning

From everything and nothing

You know me and I know you

When you linger, swallowing

From me, you're feeding

YOU

There so many people

In this world

But it's that special combination of traits

That you possess

That makes you glow blue

In a planet overrun by red flames

VOYAGE

Join me

In my fairy tale

Keep me company

Be my companion in hell

And we won't be stopped

From what's coming

Not only, we will be free

But we will be kings

We are ones in rising

Our time is coming

Follow me

In the scorching flames

In my sanctuary

We'll bring Sanity to fail

And we won't be stopped

From what's coming

Not only, we will be free

But we will be kings

We are ones in rising

Our time is coming

Our time is coming

Our time is coming

We won't be stopped

From what's coming

Not only, we will be free

But we will be kings

We are ones in rising

Our time is coming

Our time is coming

Our time is coming

Our time is coming

WATER

No one should cry
Then wipe your tears
If you long for something better
Then you should know
That even in the dark
There is always a hint of light
In between those sobs
That drench you dry

See, a pool at your feet ,
But not far, the muds are turning green
Your eyelids always seem to be pulled down
But flowers won't stop blowing around you

Your couch is warm but your body is cold
You can still complain but the truth is that
Water, you don't need no more
All this is getting old

Now is the time to wake up

Life at it's fullest to enjoy

The searing nervousness to overcome

The palette of people to get to known

And undefined things to learn from

Do not shy away from what's yours to take

Opportunities my dear never last

Fly like a butterfly

Forge your own nest

See, a pool at your feet ,

But not far, the muds are turning green

Your eyelids always seem to be pulled down

But flowers won't stop blowing around you

Your couch is warm but your body is cold
You can still complain but the truth is that
Water, you don't need no more
All this is getting old

Soon you will be able to reach the stars
Because in your own way
You glitter, you spark

CYCLES

There is always a time
When you feel useless
A night to avoid sleep
A moment in life
When you feel the lowest
But still, you'll have this

Then comes again the reminiscing
The lack of shoulders to lean
On, and on there is trying
The wants to share
To give and (to) have
And the thought (that) you're always mocked

No matter what you do
You feel poor, so poor inside
No matter what you say
It still hurts to breathe yet you sigh

No matter what you grieve

You cannot do but silence it
Because you hold one of the best life
But there's always the wonder
Of what's there to hold on

There's always something
For you to wait
But not always a reward
For you to get

So much things to work hard
For (with) nothing to obtain
But you'll still have this

Then there's often moments you're enjoying
Not matter how hard it's to understand
The world you're living in

The little things that gets you exited

You crave to experience them
But then you are left to starve

No matter what you do
You feel poor, so poor inside
No matter what you say
It still hurts to breathe yet you sigh
No matter what you grieve

You cannot do but silence it
Because you hold one of these

The luxury of health

But there's always the wonder

Of what's there to hold on

Guess there's not much to see

Guess there's nowhere to be

But to yield to the motion

No flames to bring

No love to carry on

Just to walk until

Your last breathe comes

GAMBLING

You want to play a little longer
But what will you gain
The thing is, you're not a good gambler
And your life is at stake

You don't know what you wonder
You don't know what you feel
You don't know where to start
But you got yourself a bargain

So launch the dice
Watch it turn, turn
Round and round
Keep on grabbing
The edge of your tousled bangs

Surely it makes you go wild

Frustrated to no end

But this is your own making

This is your game

Now you really get what it is to live

Thy mixed émotions playing you

Like a chord on a string

Stretched, pulled and everything in between

But you can't get it out of under your skin

Thought you had ringing alarms

You've never been one to listen

Instinct is doing the call

And for once you're caving in

Letting yourself get loose

If not loosing yourself completely

But don't forget that to live once

Requires a lot of pain

In the back of your mind

Don’t forget that living once

Requires to feel some of the pain

BREAKING UP

You must have been smoking something
To find yourself in this state
I don't want to be seen with you
Baby, you missed something
And that won't do

Keep saying
That you are « Head over heels »
More for the drink, you confessed
Than for this mess
Cheaper and more easy to impress

Good for your wealth
Still bad for your breath
For once you reek
So forget about that kiss

It's about time

You get a new pair of shoes

A little to big ?

They fit all right

With the size of your ego

Wipe those stains of booze

Be careful

You might burst into a reverse hero

For that was the final straw

I'm breaking up with you

For that was the final straw

I'm getting rid of you

PERFECT

I ain't perfect

And I'll never be what you want me to be

I don't deserve it

But I'm hoping one day I'll be free

I'll keep on searching

Finding what's meant for me

My heart full of love but it's easy to break

I'll give all you want but it's easy to take

Don't take it all take it all for granted

If you love me don't hurt me

My heart can't take more damage

I hide my tears behind this smile

But sometimes my mask becomes see through

Bit of me starts to leak through

Don't pity me

I'm no fool

HOW TO LET YOU GO

To get rid of this emotion
After that we met
Now how to move with caution
With no fraction of regrets

Discerning real feeling
From lust sweet nest
Stop ending being greedy
Should come out of this trance

But your pull, it gets to much
And fighting it is so hard
It push out all my weaknesses
It breaks all of my efforts

And you're always on my mind
You're always on my mind
And I don't know how to let you go

You could do what you want of me

But I'll always come beg

Beg you not to spit me out, my baby

That would make me go so mad

You wouldn't want me to be scary

And I wouldn't want to turn out like Carrie

No, you're always on my mind

You're always on my mind

And I don't know how to let you go

How to let you go ?

Already my darling, how to let you go ?

My baby, how to let you go ?

How would I ever get a chance ? When I love you so

And you're always on my mind

You're always on my mind

And I don’t know how to let you go

IN VAIN

He likes to talk a lot
He doesn't do much
He wants to be tough
But got no strength at all

He likes to be the big man
But have no use of his brain
He relishes in the vain
To forget he is nothing but plain

He is the master of avoidance
When you turn the facts on him
He tends to sneer at the evidence
He lives to put pain as pain was put on him

He lacks no confidence
It is like a second skin he's wearing
But he has no substance

He perpetuates the art of smashing

He toys with feelings
He knows, are devastating
It is his kryptonite
To forget he was nothing but stain
He is the master of avoidance

When you turn the facts on him
He tends to sneer at the evidence
He lives to put pain as pain was put on him

He relishes in the vain
To forget he is nothing but plain

When he bleeds within the walls
He swore to never show what's there to crack
He wants to be the one on the top
To feel others at his mercy
Kissing his shoes licking his toes like he was the King

To make it more real

He is acting the part

He seethees to discard those

Who treated him with no disregard

He fed from it for so long

Now he wouldn't stop

He is in too deep

It is under his skin

He knows more vain

That he knows himself

He knows more vain

Because he is in pain

TAINTED BLACK

Here they call me crazy
They don't know what to do with me
In my head they try to creep
But defense I bleed

Why vowing to turn me mad
Stepping on whose sides
Quenching vile stories to feed
Once there is no coming back

Why planting seed
There is no heart to steel
When I'll loose my mind
There is no coming back

Before my doorstep they hide
Those red-tapped files
Me and my dark thoughts

We are not in peace

Why vowing to turn me mad
Stepping on whose sides
Quenching vile stories to feed
Once there is no coming back

Why make me a slave to breed
There is no heart to steel
When I'll loose my mind
There is no coming back

Let them they think they know
What's whirling around in here
For them to leave me alone
I'll do the necessary

They do not have to know that
In here everything is black

They must not know that

I am tainted black

VERIDIS

Damnation

I lost my cool again

And out of frustration

I've thrown caution to the air

Thus I spilled over

What was in my heart

But you're one to blame

You had total control

Over my reaction

For every tears I've cried

Over you every day

Don't you worry

I will make youp ay

For everything

You made me go through

Don't you worry

I will give it back to you

And I thought between us

The connection was strong

Guess who was wrong ?

But now it's a fair game

Don't mind if I stall

What's that they say ?

That what goes around comes around

I promise by the time i twill end

You'll know frustration

For every tears I've cried

Over you every day

Don't you worry

I will make you pay

For everything

You made me go through

Don't you worry

I will give it back to you

LIFE GOES ON

Try to remember sometimes

That your skin and bone

Make it harder on ourselves

Than It needs to be

And I can't remember the last time

That changed anything

It's always been life or death to me

That's how it needs to be

It's overwhelming sometimes

When you're all alone

And you can't tell if you're floating or falling out of place

Like the astronaut calls a little dot a home

Like he can tell from out

LATE NIGHT DREAMS

It would be a dream

To lay by your side tonight

And see your skin gleam

In the bedside table's light

If you're afraid of love

You'll never be kissed

If you're afraid to leave

You'll never be missed

Don't lose your softness

For the world is harsh enough

It has only shown and taught us

It is a fallacy to act as rough

Since being soft isn't really a mistake

For in life only hard things easily break

PEACE

I put these words into the universe and hope the people listen

Felt like I hit the end of my worth , my soul was distant

Love was missing

I needed something to boost my ambition

The weight of the world on my chest

I needed something uplifting

I found peace while writing these verses

Questioning my coexistence with life

There was same queues

I missed them

BOOMERANG

I always come back to this
I always come back to you

God grant me

The serenity to accept,

Courage to change,
Wisdom to know

The difference.

FEELING FREE

You don't tie me up

In Knots

Like you used to

And it feels so free

In slowly,

I'm unfolding.

IN MEMORY

We are very few things

And we must take advantage of every second,

Every minute here below

You knew how to do a lot with so little

You who knew how to cultivate love and friendship.

You made these moments

Rare and so appreciable

How to forget them ?

How can you forget the faithful and generous person

The beloved cousin and friend,

The caring father that you have always been ?

Impossible

Your memory will always be engraved in our hearts.

We will only have to remember your laughter,

Your good humor,

Your kindness and your eternal optimism.

Love you forever Brayane.

J'AURAIS ...

J'aurais aimé te dire davantage que j'étais désolé
d'avoir brisé ton cœur

Et le mien par la même occasion

J'aurais aimé te serrer dans mes bras une dernière
fois,

T'aimer encore un peu,

Avant de te dire adieu

J'aurais préféré t'avouer que je n'arrivais plus à
avancer sans toi,

Plutôt que de laisser les mots mourir en moi

J'aurais aimé te crier de ne plus partir,

Te dire de m'attendre parce que j'avais encore
besoin de toi

J'aurais aimé te dire un peu plus tôt que je t'aimais encore,

Que je t'aimais toujours,

Que je n'avais jamais cessé de le faire malgré tout le mal que je t'ai fait.

Je t'aimerais toujours ...

WHAT LOVE IS

So hard to forgot pain

But it's even harder to remember sweetness and love .

We have no scar to show for happiness.

I want love to be simple

I want to trust without thinking

I want tot be generous with my affection and patience

And love unconditionnally.

I want to love the whole person,

Not the parts

And this is how I want to be loved

www.ingramcontent.com/pod-product-compliance
Lightning Source LLC
LaVergne TN
LVHW091027150826
845672LV00006BA/1718

* 9 7 9 8 4 5 9 6 3 0 0 2 2 *